Imagining
the Past

11 A Victorian Factory Town

Philip Sauvain

Illustrated by Trevor Ridley

- 2 Introduction
- 4 Entering a Factory town
- 6 The Railway Station
- 8 Busy Streets
- 10 Street Traders and Entertainers
- 12 In the Back Streets
- 14 A Worker's Home
- 16 At Work
- 18 Going Shopping
- 20 At School
- 22 In Chapel
- 24 Entertainments
- 26 In the Park
- 28 The Workhouse
- 30 Time Line
- 31 Things to Do

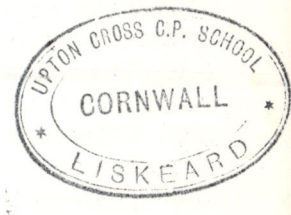

Macmillan Education

Introduction

The building of factories and works using iron machines and steam power from coal was the most striking thing about Britain in the eighteenth and nineteenth centuries. In 1700 there were very few mills or works employing large numbers of people. Only a few towns and villages were really industrial. By 1900, two hundred years later, Britain was the most important industrial nation in the world. The United States, Germany, and later Russia and Japan, were to overtake her in due course, but in Victorian times British industry was well in advance of the rest of the world.

Many new towns had developed out of small hamlets such as Middlesbrough, Crewe and Swindon. Barrow-in-Furness had 150 people in the 1840s and 60,000 in the 1890s. Many older towns and villages changed rapidly as new factories and mills were built. Row after row of terraced houses were built so that the industrial workers could live near their work. People in country areas moved into the towns because there were jobs there. Improvements in living conditions meant that people and particularly children, lived longer. The population grew rapidly.

If you could have seen a Victorian factory town in the middle of the nineteenth century you would have been surprised at the amount of new building in progress. New houses and new public buildings were everywhere. Railway stations were built in

the 1840s and 1850s and this also meant railway lines, sheds, sidings and new hotels. People liked to live near a railway station. The railway was a cheap and very convenient form of transport. An industrial worker could take his family on the train to the seaside on Bank Holiday Monday. Streets of terraced houses were built near the railway stations in most towns. This was one of the main areas where towns tended to grow in the nineteenth century. Another area of growth was near the mills and factories.

Many of these Victorian houses can still be seen today. In most of the important Victorian factory towns it is possible to imagine what it was like to live in this period of great change. Town halls, hospitals, churches, chapels, banks, shops and many other buildings show the amount of new building then. Today many public buildings have been cleaned and the original colour of the stone can be seen. In Victorian times they were covered with soot. Victorian factory towns were unpleasant places to live in. They were dirty and noisy. The atmosphere was filled with smoke and soot. The rivers were used to carry waste from the mills.

The photograph shows part of Huddersfield seen from a hill and the picture above shows Sheffield as it looked to an artist in 1874.

Entering a Factory Town

If you catch a bus today on the outskirts of a big industrial town with many Victorian buildings, such as Barnsley, Blackburn or Gateshead, you will often find that your bus ride takes you on a journey back in time. The nearer you get to the centre of the town, the further back in time you go. If you look closely you can pick out the old buildings and see how they differ from the new. The journey from the fringe of the town may start in an area where there are fields and woods, and houses built in the 1960s. As the bus goes towards the centre of town earlier houses built in the 1950s, 1930s and 1920s come into view. Soon taller houses, particularly semi-detached homes with bay windows, and house and street names such as Alexandra Street, can be seen. These are buildings erected in the last years of the nineteenth and the early years of the twentieth centuries (when Edward VII was King and Alexandra his Queen). You are now on the edge of the Victorian town. This was where the countryside began in 1900. You may see large detached houses, like small mansions, with tall rounded windows reminding you of church windows and maybe turrets like those on a castle.

Well-to-do people in Victorian times could afford to live some distance from the centre of the town away from the noise, the factory smells and the smoke. They had private carriages to take them to work. The better-off workers could also afford to live some way out and catch the horse bus into town. In the last years of the nineteenth century horse trams, and later electric trams, provided an even cheaper form of travel. But the ordinary worker could only afford to walk to work.

The street names give a clue to their age since they are often named after people who were famous at the time, or after notable events such as Omdurman Road, Rosebery Avenue and Gladstone Terrace. Nearer the centre of town there are even older and plainer terraced houses with street names from the middle years of the nineteenth century such as Peel Street and Albert Terrace. This is an area of mills, factories, canals and the railway station. The houses were not so well-built and are often small and close to one another. For this reason many have been pulled down and replaced by blocks of flats. But the old street names often remain.

At last you reach the town centre. Nowadays there is probably a modern shopping centre here, but if you look carefully you will see some Victorian buildings such as chapels, banks, shops, arcades, the town hall, public baths and buildings erected for special purposes, such as a Corn Exchange.

The Railway Station

The first passenger railway service was opened in 1830. Trains ran between Liverpool and Manchester and were pulled by steam locomotives like the 'Locomotion' engine seen in the photograph opposite. This locomotive is on view at the open air museum at Beamish in County Durham. In the 1830s and 1840s hundreds of railway stations were opened and new lines were built criss-crossing Britain and linking every place of importance. The coming of the railway brought new jobs and new business to the towns.

The railway station was built as close as possible to the centre of the town but since there were already many other buildings in the important towns, it was often cheaper for the new railway companies to buy land on the edge of the town, rather than land which was already used for housing. In London the great northern railway stations of King's Cross, Euston and Paddington, all lie roughly on the edge of London as it was before the middle of the nineteenth century. Later stations such as Charing Cross and Liverpool Street involved the clearance of existing housing. Old medieval towns like Norwich, Ipswich, Chester, Bristol, York and Cambridge almost invariably have railway stations which are some distance away from the centre of the modern town. Towns which grew because of the coming of the railway often have stations close to the town centre, such as in Swindon or in the seaside resorts of Blackpool, Morecambe and Ramsgate. At Brighton, which had grown in the Regency period, the station is a long walk from the sea front. Many industrial towns which were greatly helped by the railway also have stations close to the town centre such as Newcastle upon Tyne (shown in the photograph), Huddersfield, Leeds and Middlesbrough. Middlesbrough was a hamlet of 150 people in 1830 and a busy town of 90,000 people in 1901.

In Victorian times the scene around a newly-built station was a hive of activity. Streets were being erected, deep trenches dug, temporary huts put up and piles of bricks, scaffolding and giant cranes were everywhere. Many railway stations have altered little from the days when they were built. The railway traveller in about 1860 could have paid for his ticket at a booking office very similar to many seen today. He might have crossed the same footbridge to the same platform and glanced at the same station clock. At the bookstall he could have bought the daily or evening newspaper or found a book to read. If the train was not due in immediately he could have gone to the Refreshment Room.

Travellers' complaints were the same then as they often are today! His luggage might have been left at the Luggage Room and if he had lost anything he could always look for it at Lost Luggage. Notice Boards indicated the times of arrival and departure and if there was time to spare he could always wait in a waiting room. Indeed, the Victorian railway station looked very much like the modern station apart from the steam locomotives and carriages on the lines and the hansom cabs waiting outside.

Busy Streets

Once outside the railway station the modern visitor to a town in Victorian times would have noticed big differences in the streets leading to the town centre. There were no road signs or markings on the cobbled roads and the busy streets were everywhere dominated by the horse-drawn vehicle. You could catch a bus but it was drawn by a horse. The horse bus was introduced into England in 1829 by George Shillibeer. It had a coachman as driver and a conductor (sometimes known as the 'cad') standing on a ledge at the back. The cad took the fares, told the driver when to stop and urged would-be passengers to get on his bus rather than those of rival conductors. Passengers were squashed into the seats inside and squeezed up during the rush hour when the cad tried to get as many paying customers as possible into his bus.

The horse buses were single deckers at first but it was soon realised that seats could be placed on the roof of the bus as well. In the 1850s these seats were back-to-back on a bench which ran the length of the bus (sometimes called the 'knife-board'). In the 1880s the seats were placed across the width of the bus so that the passengers then faced the way they were going.

The traveller who decided to take a cab from the station could often choose between the slow but steady four-wheeled cab which was known as a *growler* or the faster two-wheeled hansom cab which was more manoeuvrable, but more likely to be involved in an accident. The driver of the growler sat in front on a box whilst the hansom cab driver sat perched up behind the cab containing the passenger. In the 1860s you might also have been able to catch a horse tram and after 1885 there were electric trams in some towns. It was now possible to travel cheaply from one part of a town to another. Other traffic on the streets included heavy horse-drawn waggons piled as high as the second storey of a house and huge brewers' drays laden with barrels of beer.

There were no petrol filling stations but there were horse troughs at the sides of the streets. Traffic jams often occurred with horse buses, cabs, carriages, cattle, pedestrians, waggons and donkey carts at a standstill. In London, policemen sometimes directed traffic in the trouble spots. There were traffic islands but no safety crossings for pedestrians. These islands had lamp standards to light the centre of the road, bollards to protect pedestrians standing there and sometimes Keep Left signs high up on one of the lamp standards. The only street crossings were those where crossing sweepers armed with brushes swept a clean path across the dirty street soiled by horse droppings. There were no traffic wardens, and drivers parked their vehicles where they wished. To add to these troubles people often complained because the road was up! Road works were frequent since many new sewers, drains, gas pipes, water mains, telephone wires and electricity cables were laid in the later years of the century.

Street Traders and Entertainers

The modern visitor to a Victorian town or city would have been surprised by the crowds to be seen in the streets. Most Victorian families were very big. Ten children was not particularly large by Victorian standards. Queen Victoria herself had nine children. Before 1870 it was not compulsory to go to school and during the day there were lots of children on the streets. There were many more poor people in those days and no unemployment pay to provide food for those who were out of work. Poor children tried to scrape a living by scavenging for food, brushing a path across the streets as crossing sweepers or simply by begging.

There were many street traders and delivery men. Wages were very low and many people took up trades which nowadays would not be worthwhile. Shoes were cleaned by shoeshine boys in the centres of most towns. Outside a railway station there were men with trays selling balloons or trays of matches, small toys and other goods. Newsboys, flower-sellers, costermongers selling fruit from a barrow, street-sellers of ice cream (sometimes called hokey-pokey), barrow boys with fried fish, hot eels, hot green peas, ginger beer, lemonade, hot pies, sandwiches, hot chestnuts and almost every type of food or product filled the streets of the busy city. Men with sandwich boards advertised shops by walking up and down the pavements. We know a lot about their activities from the writings of a man called Henry Mayhew who interviewed thousands of street folk (as he called them) in the 1840s and 1850s.

Street entertainers played every type of musical instrument from the guitar and the tom-tom to the bagpipes and the barrel organ. The organ grinders or hurdy-gurdy men, as they were sometimes called, were on every street corner playing the latest tunes. Many people gave them money to encourage them to go away! Acrobats, jugglers, clowns, tightrope walkers, conjurors, fire-eaters, dancing dogs, performing monkeys (often accompanying the organ grinder) and especially the Punch and Judy Show were street entertainments which were popular at a time when there was no radio or television or cinema. The streets of the Victorian town echoed with sounds and noises. A man in a balloon high above London said the thing he noticed most of all was the perpetual roar from the city spread out below him.

In the Back Streets

The street traders were to be seen in the back streets as well as in the busy centre of the town. There were costermongers selling fruit and vegetables, rag-and-bone men, men who bought old clothes or umbrellas or rags; there were people who went from door to door offering to repair chairs, mend clocks, remove grease from clothes or grind knives. The milkman brought round milk in a churn and filled jugs at the houses on his list. There were no milk bottles or cartons. On a regular round his horse followed him down the street as he went from door to door – something a modern electric milk float is unable to do! The coalman emptied coal directly into the cellar through a hole in the pavement. These coal hole covers can sometimes be seen in the streets today. The muffin man brought round fresh muffins at tea-time and the beerman called to fill your jug with beer in the evening.

The main streets of the town were lit by gas lamps at the start of the century and by electric lighting in some towns by the 1890s. Water supply was often primitive in the early years of Queen Victoria's reign. In some streets one tap was turned on for twenty minutes a day only and had to serve a whole neighbourhood. Some people lived several hundred metres from a tap. The drains and the sewers were often in appalling condition. An inspector reported on streets in Manchester in the 1850s with comments such as 'filthy black drainage . . . bad stench . . . most abominable privies (lavatories) . . . privies very dreadful'. In one Manchester street twenty homes shared five privies and two wells. Victorian slums were gloomy, broken-down buildings with shattered windows covered with rags or paper, broken shutters and doors. Many of these homes were so crowded, whole families would live and sleep in one small room with bare floorboards and one or two broken chairs. We know this because artists at the time drew pictures of typical scenes, such as the houses of Lancashire cotton workers in the 1860s. Writers like Charles Dickens frequently described the terrible living conditions of the poor in their stories.

Many of these slum houses were situated on damp ground close to a river. The marshland at the bottom of a valley was cheap and the manufacturer who built the houses for his workers also wanted them to live close to his mill or factory. This had been built at the riverside to be near water for the steam engines and because waste materials could be emptied into the river. Dense factory smoke, the noise and smell of the machines and the filthy rivers helped to make conditions in the slums even worse. Some of these areas were cleared in Victorian towns and there were many improvements in later years as drains, gas and electricity supplies, mains water and new road surfaces were provided.

A Worker's Home

Most of the slums of the Victorian factory towns have been cleared. Many of those that remain are derelict like the houses in Middlesbrough shown in the photograph, and these will eventually be cleared and either replaced by new buildings or grassed over. Most of the slums of today were thought to be good homes in Victorian times. At that time few workers' houses had bathrooms, inside lavatories, separate kitchens or even hot and cold running water or an oven. The worker who counted himself well-off lived in a small terraced house with perhaps one or two rooms downstairs and one or two rooms upstairs (sometimes called 'two up and two down'). The terrace usually opened out directly on to the street or into a small paved yard where the privy was situated in a shed.

Many houses were built round a court or courtyard where the families shared a privy and a water tap with their neighbours. In the courtyard you would have seen washing strung across a line and perhaps women busy with their dolly tubs. They were always busy with the dolly tub. This was a barrel in which a wooden stick with a flat end could be thumped up and down to get the washing clean.

There were no modern soaps or detergents, of course. Many wives had to go out to work themselves, working as millhands or even in collieries hauling coal tubs. It was not work they could enjoy.

Meals were very simple. Breakfast for a cotton worker in the 1840s was porridge, bread and milk. Lunch was bread, bacon and potatoes. Tea was bread, butter and tea. If supper was served it was again porridge or potatoes and milk. On Sundays there might have been a joint of meat. Few families had a cooker so the meat was taken to the baker's shop and cooked in his oven. When it was taken out into the street the small joint of mutton or beef was often surrounded by 'a vast heap of half-browned potatoes' and a family of eager children danced round it 'for very joy at the prospect of the feast'. A family of six living in the 1890s was said by the writer Charles Booth to have existed on about 17s 5d (87p) a week. Every time they needed tea and sugar they went to the corner shop to buy 'a pinch'.

Families had to fight a constant battle to keep clean. Even the front doorstep of many a house in northern England was kept spotless by using a donkey stone (a piece of yellow stone which was used to scrape the surface). Since the streets were dirty, the atmosphere sooty and the mill or factory full of dust, grime and oil, it was heartbreaking for the housewife.

At Work

The old mills and factories of the Victorian period are often to be seen in towns today, although few are working as they did a hundred years ago. Many gloomy warehouses and eight-storeyed mills have been converted to other uses and some house a number of small modern factories within the one building. Only in one or two towns, and in one or two industries, is it still possible to see the chimneys smoking as they did in Victorian times. Some people worried by the likelihood that all traces of the buildings and machines used in Victorian times may be lost, have banded together to form groups known as industrial archaeologists. They hope to preserve and keep in good working order some of the interesting relics of our industrial past. Old collieries (see photograph opposite top) can be visited and old tramways and old steam locomotives can be seen at open-air museums, such as those at Beamish in County Durham, Ironbridge in Shropshire or at the Crich Tramway Museum in Derbyshire.

Working conditions in the mines and mills of the early nineteenth century were grim. The day began early in a terraced street in a textile town. The knocker-up went round with a long pole rattling on bedroom windows and waking millworkers and their families at 4.00 or 5.00 a.m. In the 1840s a writer called Douglas Jerrold described a typical scene. 'It is five o'clock on a

January morning. The child is up, and with its scanty covering pulled about it, descends shivering to the street.' In the mill she suffered 'the racking noise of engines' all day long and 'the dragging, wearying monotony of the machine; the stifling heat; the unbroken noise.' The smell of the oil used to grease the engines was everywhere and in a cotton mill small fibres of cotton were gulped in at every breath. After a long day of work the child fell asleep immediately to be woken again by the rattle on the window and the clatter of clogs (wooden shoes) on the cobbled streets outside as the workers went back to the mill once again.

Many children died in accidents. Pit explosions were frequent. As you can see from the photograph of a monument in the churchyard at Silkstone near Barnsley in Yorkshire, many children worked underground in Victorian times. Factory regulations gradually improved conditions in the mills and pits but even in 1900 they were still poor.

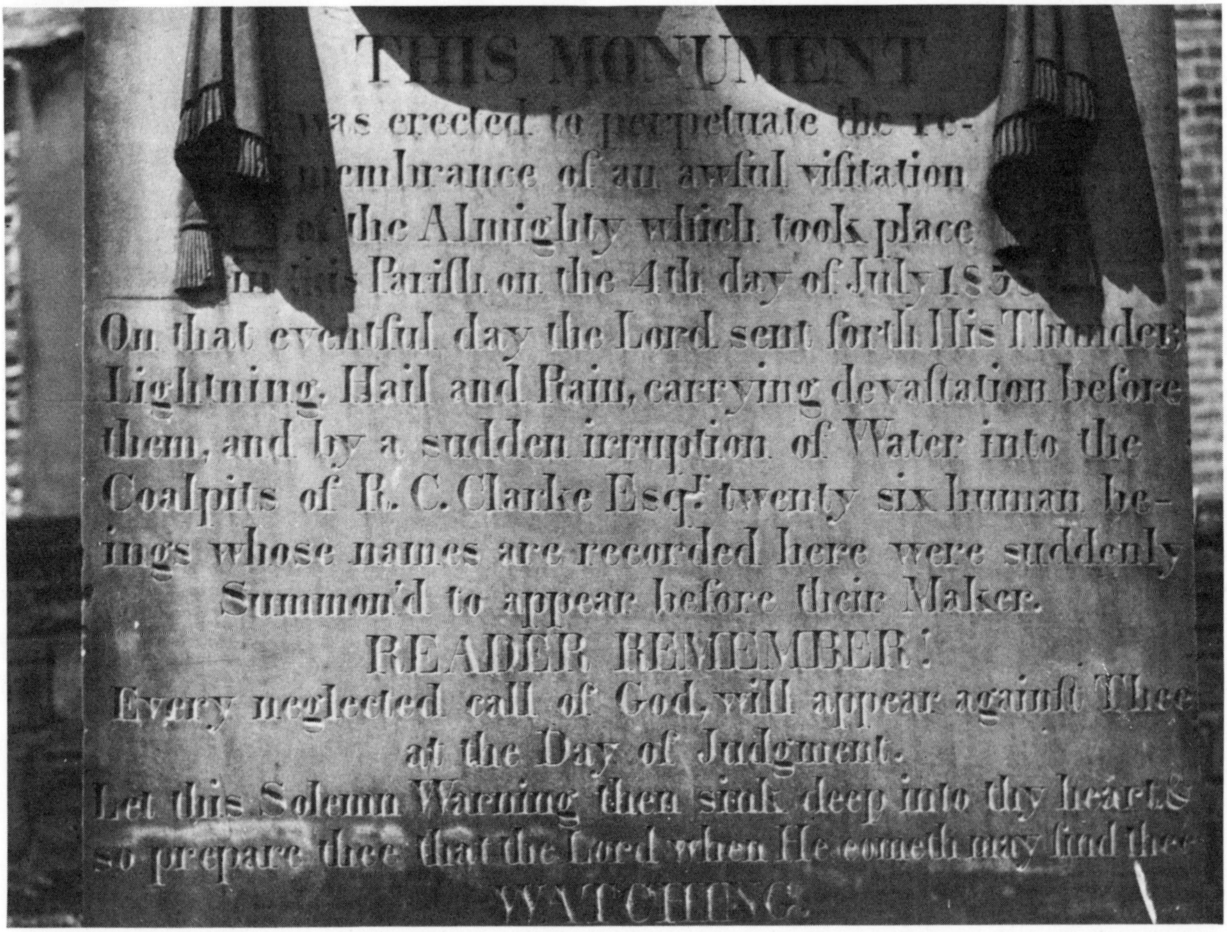

THIS MONUMENT
was erected to perpetuate the re-
membrance of an awful visitation
of the Almighty which took place
in this Parish on the 4th day of July 1838
On that eventful day the Lord sent forth His Thunder
Lightning, Hail and Rain, carrying devastation before
them, and by a sudden irruption of Water into the
Coalpits of R. C. Clarke Esq! twenty six human be-
ings whose names are recorded here were suddenly
Summon'd to appear before their Maker.
READER REMEMBER!
Every neglected call of God will appear against Thee
at the Day of Judgment.
Let this Solemn Warning then sink deep into thy hearts
so prepare thee that the Lord when He cometh may find thee
WATCHING.

Going Shopping

The shop names in the centre of a Victorian factory town were almost always those of local tradesmen. There were few chain stores and the first department store was not open in Britain until 1863 (it was called the Universal Provider). W. H. Smith and his son were still building up their newsagents business, especially the bookstalls they were opening on railway stations. Jesse Boot started his chemist's shop in Nottingham in 1877, whilst Frank Winfield Woolworth opened his first store in the U.S.A. in 1879, although it was not until 1910 that a branch of Woolworths was opened in Britain. There were co-operative societies, however, the first co-op having been founded at Rochdale in Lancashire in 1844. Many of the businesses which were founded in the nineteenth century (and some from the eighteenth century) survive to this day although only rarely in the same shop premises. You can sometimes see the date when a shop was founded on a plaque or stone on the shop front.

The actual counters, windows and decorations used in Victorian times have usually been removed in order to modernise the shop. Sometimes it is possible to see the tiled floors and marble walls of a Victorian grocer's shop with coloured designs in mosaic patterns. Marble was cool to the touch, easily wiped and kept clean and it gave the impression that the food was being kept in cool, clean surroundings. Covered shopping areas (arcades) were often built in a similar style, as at Newcastle upon Tyne shown in the photograph. In summer, Victorian shopkeepers lowered the sunblinds outside to shade the inside of the shop and these, not necessarily the originals, can often be seen today on a hot day in June or July.

There were big window displays in Victorian shops. The small panes of the Georgian shop window had sometimes given way to large sheets of plate glass which enabled the shopkeeper to mount displays of goods which would attract the customer. Many grocers had advertisements for a product such as Cadbury's Cocoa attached permanently to the window glass. The photograph shows a grocer's shop in Bury St Edmunds in Suffolk looking much the same as it did a hundred years ago. Basket makers, shoe shops, even second-hand shops displayed much of their stock outside on the pavement. At Christmas time the butchers invariably vied with one another to put on the most impressive displays of meat with chickens, turkeys, geese, ducks, rabbits and hares hanging on lines strung out across the shop premises from ground level to the roof.

Life in the shops then was much harder for the assistants than it is today. They opened at 8.00 a.m. and usually closed at 8.00 p.m. during the week. At the weekend, when people were paid, they stayed open to 10.30 or 11.00 p.m. on Fridays and even up to midnight on Saturdays.

At School

There are still many schools with buildings which date back to the nineteenth century. In 1870 Parliament passed a law which said that School Boards had to be formed in every town and country area. These School Boards were given the power to make education compulsory for the children in their districts. If there were no Church schools already the School Boards had to provide new ones. The schools they built are usually easy to recognise today for they tended to follow the same pattern of building. You can see one such school in the photograph on this page. Most were built in the 1870s and 1880s and have a headstone or foundation stone giving details of when the school was built. The windows in these schools are often shaped like those to be seen in a church. Sometimes they have a bell tower and often a small playground surrounded by railings. Many have two gables facing the front separated by the long body of the main classroom.

Life at school in the 1870s was very hard. Discipline was strict and the teachers used the cane frequently, rapping boys and girls smartly across the knuckles or the palm of the hand. Simple mistakes were punished as well as rudeness, inattention and noisiness. The textbooks were usually dull and only a few included diagrams or pictures. Children had to write neatly in a style of writing which is called *copperplate*. It took hours of practice to write in this way. Most of the lessons were boring and monotonous, the children chanted aloud the things they had to learn. There were few trips or excursions out of school. The classes were often very large with as many as 60 or 70 pupils. Sometimes the teachers were not much older than the pupils they taught. These were the pupil-teachers who started to teach when they reached the age of 13.

In Chapel

As the number of people in the towns grew rapidly in the nineteenth century, new churches and chapels were built, and many were designed to look like medieval churches. The most important change however, was the building of thousands of chapels, churches and meeting houses by groups of Methodists, Congregationalists, Baptists, Unitarians, the Salvation Army and others. The growth of Methodism (see *Imagining the Past: Book 9*) was partly due to the fact that the new method of worship could be easily understood by people who had not been to school. In the chapel, many of the preachers were working men themselves during the week and so were able to use stories about their working lives in mills or collieries in their sermons. But factory workers often felt uneasy in church. Henry Mayhew met a Londoner in 1850 who said, 'I never goes to any church or chapel. Sometimes I hasn't clothes as is fit, and I suppose I couldn't be admitted into such fine places in my working dress. They're fittest for rich people.'

Sunday was the only day in the week when the working man was able to lie in bed in the morning, often the only occasion when he felt he and his family could afford to eat meat, and certainly the only holiday in the week. For many, these were very good reasons for not going to church on Sundays. In 1851 it was said that only two people in every five attended church or chapel. A clergyman in the 1890s said the typical working man got up between nine and ten; lingered over his breakfast, half-dressed, reading the Sunday paper; and was in the pub drinking until three before going back for Sunday dinner. On Sunday evenings many people strolled in the park and listened to the band.

Entertainments

Although most people were poorly paid throughout the nineteenth century, there were now many new ways of enjoying what leisure time there was. The seaside resorts (see *Imagining the Past: Book 12*) grew rapidly in the last years of the century. More and more people were able to go on day excursions or even take a week's holiday. There were many new music-halls. These were originally places of refreshment and the variety acts were only there to persuade the visitor to come in and spend his money on food and drink. Gradually the variety acts became more important than the refreshments. Victorian audiences were not slow to boo a performer they did not like! It became the custom to have a chairman sitting at the side of the stage, announcing the acts and keeping order. By the 1870s some of the variety acts were so popular the stars were the attraction not the food or the music hall. New variety theatres were built such as the London Hippodrome and most towns now had theatres. The variety stars of the 1880s and 1890s, such as Vesta Tilley, Marie Lloyd, Dan Leno, Little Tich and Albert Chevalier, were top of the bill wherever they appeared.

At Christmas time there were pantomimes in most towns. Other treats for children included trips to the zoo such as the Belle Vue Zoological Gardens in Manchester which were opened in 1836. Visitors there could look at the lions and monkeys (favourites in Victorian times) and then take a pleasure boat on the lake, listen to the band, find their way through the maze, have tea and go dancing in the evening.

The nineteenth century also saw the rise of professional sport. Association Football, Rugby Union and Rugby League Football were all the same game of rough-and-tumble football at the start of the nineteenth century. In the 1860s soccer and rugby separated, with the formation first of all of the Football Association (the footballers who wanted to stop players handling the ball) and then the formation of a Union of clubs who adopted the rules of football which were played at Rugby School. Later the Rugby Union split up when some northern clubs left to form a league of clubs, because they had been secretly paying some of the members of their teams (men who would otherwise have lost a day's wages from work). This was the formation of the Rugby League game. By 1900 Rugby League and Soccer were big crowd-pullers and in 1901 a record crowd of 110,000 people watched the F.A. Cup Final. Large transfer fees were already being paid and most of the modern League clubs had already been founded.

In the Park

One of the disadvantages of the growth of the factory towns was the fact that now the average person was born, grew up and worked entirely in a town area. The eighteenth-century worker had lived within sight of fields and trees. Now the fresh air was dirtied by smoke and there were frequent complaints about the yellow smoke-filled fog (often called smog today). Row after row of identical, brick, terraced houses, mill chimneys and foul rivers became the everyday world of the factory worker. Charles Dickens described Preston in the 1850s as having a black canal, an evil-smelling river and the smell of oil everywhere. Many people wanted to bring something of the country back into the towns. People who went to London saw fine parks in the centre of the city such as St James's Park, Green Park and Hyde Park. It seemed to them that the same idea could be used in their own towns. A park could provide trees, flowers and grass where ordinary people could walk and imagine themselves in the country.

In 1846 Manchester became one of the first factory towns to open a public park. Other towns opened parks within the next few years. Many of the features of the typical Victorial park can be seen today, such as a circular bandstand, an elaborate fountain, summer houses and avenues of trees. On a Victorian Sunday there were lemonade stalls with huge glass bowls of lemonade and ice-cream carts with a queue of children. Their parents could listen to the band and look at the sights. There might be soldiers in uniform, small girls with hoops, anglers at the side of a lake, boys with toy yachts, dogs on leads, children playing on the grass and young ladies in fine dresses sheltering under parasols (sun umbrellas).

The Workhouse

To many Victorians, Britain was the greatest country in the world, and if people wanted to work they could find it if they looked for it. In general they were not sympathetic to the poor. When workers were unemployed through no obvious fault of their own, the rich were sometimes prepared to help and give money to the distress funds set up to offer charity to the starving workers. When the American Civil War caused great hardship to the Lancashire cotton workers because the American cotton could not be shipped to Lancashire, there was widefelt sympathy for the families of these workers. But the idea that such money should normally come from the government was unthinkable. Only when people were so poor that otherwise they would starve to death was it necessary to take care of the really needy.

Workhouses or poor houses were built to provide such help. Many buildings had been erected in earlier times such as the workhouse at Stowmarket in Suffolk shown in the photograph. This had been built in 1777-81. It looked like a stately home from the outside but conditions inside and in all the other workhouses throughout the country were grim. The government in the 1830s felt that the poor houses or workhouses should provide a standard of living lower than that of the poorest people who had a job outside. Life in the poor house was not to be thought of as an easy way to live.

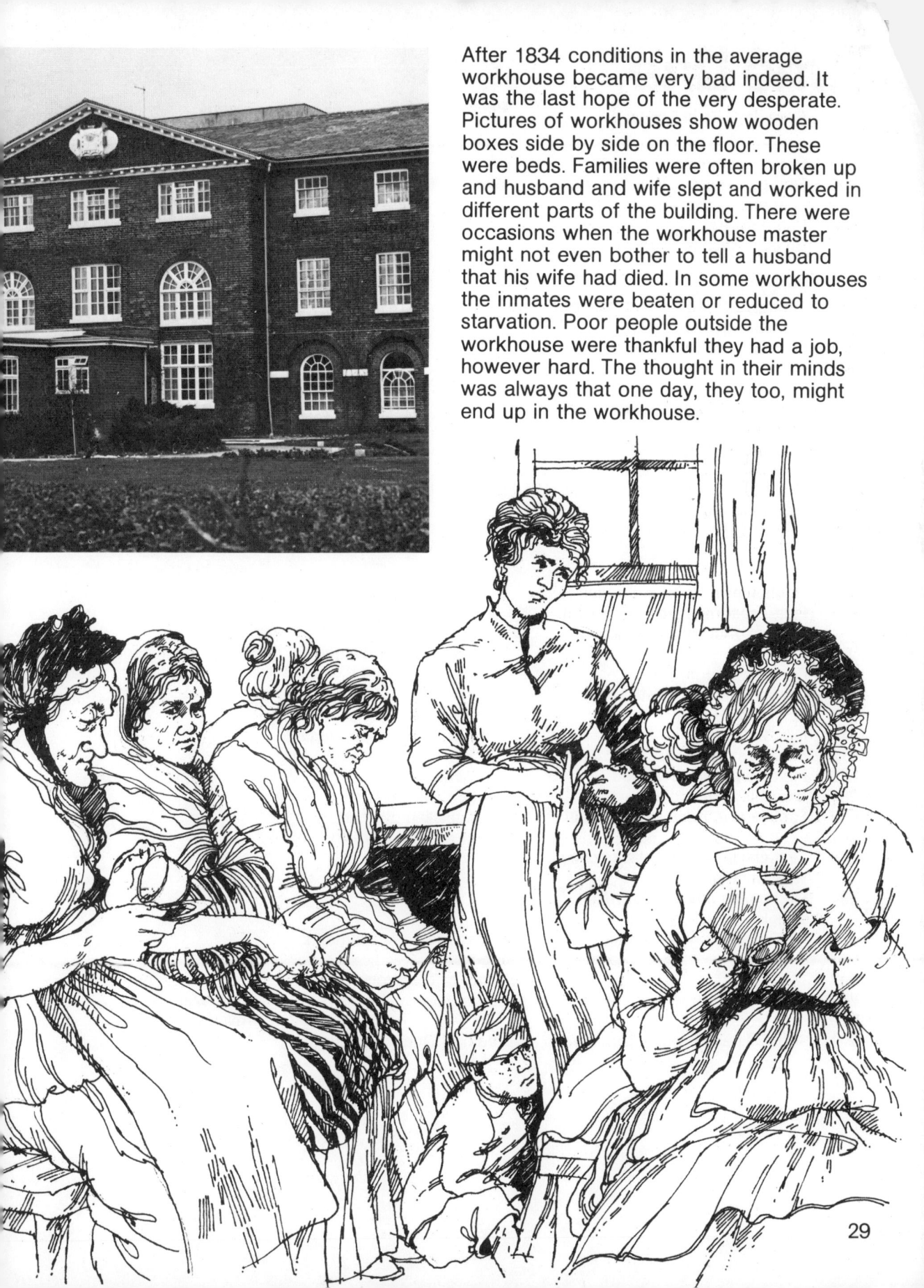

After 1834 conditions in the average workhouse became very bad indeed. It was the last hope of the very desperate. Pictures of workhouses show wooden boxes side by side on the floor. These were beds. Families were often broken up and husband and wife slept and worked in different parts of the building. There were occasions when the workhouse master might not even bother to tell a husband that his wife had died. In some workhouses the inmates were beaten or reduced to starvation. Poor people outside the workhouse were thankful they had a job, however hard. The thought in their minds was always that one day, they too, might end up in the workhouse.

Time Line

	Everyday Life in Towns	People	Events
1829	First horse buses in London		
1830	First passenger railway service	William IV is King	
1832	Outbreak of cholera		
1834	Poor Law Act Hansom cabs in London		Tolpuddle Martyrs
1837		Victoria is Queen	
1840	Penny Post		
1841	Thomas Cook organises his first rail tour		
1844	First co-op in Rochdale		
1846			Famine in Ireland
1848			Revolutions in Europe
1850	Henry Mayhew interviews London's street folk		
1851	Great Exhibition Knifeboard buses in London		
1852	First public lavatories in London	Death of Duke of Wellington	
1853	First pillar boxes		Crimean War
1854			Charge of Light Brigade
1856			End of Crimean War
1857			Indian Mutiny
1861	Horse drawn trams in London	Death of Prince Albert	American Civil War
1863	First department store in Britain Football Association formed		
1865		Death of President Lincoln	End of American Civil War
1869	Flockton Church		Opening of Suez Canal
1870	School Boards formed		
1871	First Bank Holiday	Stanley meets Livingstone	
1877	First Boots store	Victoria is Empress of India	
1878	Electric street lighting in London		
1879	First telephones in Britain	Zulu War	
1881	Shops lit by electricity	Death of Disraeli	
1885	First electric trams in Blackpool	Gordon killed at Khartoum	
1887		Queen Victoria's Golden Jubilee	
1888	First cheap working class houses with bathrooms		
1894	First motor vehicles on British streets		
1897	First motor buses in Britain	Queen Victoria's Diamond Jubilee	
1898		Death of Gladstone	Battle of Omdurman
1899			Boer War
1900			Relief of Mafeking
1901	110,000 people watch Cup Final	Death of Queen Victoria	

Things to Do

As you have seen the nineteenth century was a period of great building works. The typical Victorian factory town had many other important buildings. The Town Hall (the photograph shows Bolton Town Hall) was often built in a grand manner to show how important the town was. The design was often similar to that of a Greek or Roman temple with tall columns and an impressive flight of steps up to the main entrance. Other buildings such as a railway station or a courthouse were built in a similar way. Find out about the Victorian buildings of your town or a town nearby. Try to find out the age of buildings such as the town hall, public baths, railway station, museum, art gallery, library, and banks.

Hospitals and infirmaries often date back to Victorian times. Many towns still have a Royal Victorian Infirmary (often known by its initials R.V.I.). In Victorian hospital scenes wards are shown with beds on either side, curtains screening patients, chairs for visitors, flowers and bedside cabinets. Many hospital wards still look like this but of course the modern hospital is very different from the R.V.I. of the late nineteenth century. Make a list of the ways in which Victorian hospitals have changed.

What Victorian features are shown in the photographs? Draw pictures of them in use about ninety years ago.

Index

accidents 17
cads 8
dolly tub 14
electric trams 4, 8
entertainments 10, 24
food 14
growler 8
hansom cab 7, 8
horse bus 4, 8
horse tram 4, 8
industry 2, 16
parks 26
railways 3, 4, 6
religion 22
schools 20
shops 18
slums 12, 14
sport 24
Time Line 30
traders 10, 12
variety theatre 24
waggons 8
workhouse 28

© 1979 Philip Sauvain
Illustrations © 1979 Macmillan Education Ltd
Published by Macmillan Education Ltd,
London and Basingstoke

First published 1979

Printed in Hong Kong